Whoa!
slow down for a
moment with God

Devotions
inspired
by the beauty
of horses

Whoa! slow down for a moment with God
ISBN 978-0-9848369-3-2

Published by Product Concept Mfg., Inc.
2175 N. Academy Circle #200, Colorado Springs, CO 80909

All scripture quotations are from the King James version
of the Bible unless otherwise noted.

Scriptures taken from the Holy Bible,
New International Version®, NIV®.
Copyright © 1973, 1978, 1984 by Biblica, Inc.™
Used by permission of Zondervan.
All rights reserved worldwide.
www.zondervan.com

Sayings not having a credit listed are contributed by writers
for Product Concept Mfg., Inc. or in a rare case,
the author is unknown.

Written and Compiled by Patricia Mitchell
in association with Product Concept Mfg., Inc.

Whoa!
slow down for a moment with God

There is something about the outside
of a horse that is good for the inside of a man.

Winston Churchill

Horses have touched the spirit of humankind for thousands of years. They have been prized for their speed and bravery, for their loyalty and companionship, and for their sheer magnificence. Who could fail to feel a thrill of adventure while watching these splendid creatures as they gallop freely across an open field?

Whoa! Slow down for a moment with God is a collection of entertaining stories, uplifting readings, and inspiring quotations designed for anyone who admires horses. With warmth and humor, these thoughts encourage you to reflect on all the things you have always admired about horses—the horses you have met in books, those you have seen on TV and in films, and the special ones you have owned, ridden, and loved.

Whoa! Let yourself slow down for a moment with some of God's most amazing, fascinating, and marvelous creatures...and for a moment with Him!

*The grace, beauty, and sweet tempera-
ment of a well-trained horse attest to the
affection and expertise of his trainers. Like
each one of us, horses possess unique per-
sonalities and have different talents and
abilities. Just as we appreciate the person
who takes time to get to know us, understand our struggles, and help us through
our difficulties, so do our equine friends.*

*With regular, day-to-day interaction, a
horse learns to trust his human handlers,
and their willingness to understand his
needs before they insist on their own
gives the horse confidence and security.
When an animal consistently experiences
patience and kindness from his trainers,
he'll readily accept their guidance and
direction. He's eager to please, and will
give them his best effort.*

*As long as the human heart doesn't give
up on the horse, he won't want to give up
on us.*

Hold On!

Has an obstacle ever caused you to quit? It has happened to most of us at one time or another. The experience can either undermine our confidence in our ability to succeed, or make us determined not to let the next bump in the road throw us off balance. From life's challenges, we grow either more fearful or more persistent.

Persistence is something God possesses in abundance. He's persistent when it comes to loving us, strengthening us, and supporting us. He never gets tired of helping us up after we've fallen and showing us where to find the good of any situation. He always will be there to lead us over, around, or through life's rough spots, no matter how big they may appear to our eyes.

God's love for you never quits, and from Him you have the confidence you need to hold on when the ride gets rough!

When my confidence fails me, dear God,
remind me of the strength I have in You.
Enable me to keep holding on! Amen

When you get into a tight place
and everything goes against you,
till it seems as though you could not
hold on a minute longer, never give
up then, for that is just the place
and time that the tide will turn.
Harriet Beecher Stowe

Riding is the art of keeping a horse
between you and the ground.
Author unknown

We know that suffering produces
perseverance; perseverance,
character; and character, hope.
And hope does not disappoint us,
because God has poured out his love
into our hearts by the Holy spirit,
whom he has given us.
Romans 5:3-5 NIV

You must do the thing
you think you cannot do.
Eleanor Roosevelt

The race is not always to the swift,
but to those who keep on running.
Saying

*The block of granite which was an
obstacle in the pathway of the weak
becomes a stepping stone in the
pathway of the strong.*
Thomas Carlyle

**This one thing I do, forgetting those
things which are behind, and reach-
ing forth unto those things which are
before, I press toward the mark for
the prize of the high calling of
God in Christ Jesus.**
Philippians 3:13-14

*I think that if I become a horseman,
I shall be a man on wings.*
Xenophon

**Emotions, like fiery stallions,
are powerful and strong. Yet only
with training and teaching does their
power prove useful, fruitful,
and of lasting value.**
Author unknown

*No great deed is done by falterers
who ask for certainty.*
George Eliot

Every day on his way to work, Ed would take the road that bordered the brown colt's pasture fence. The animal's listless eyes would follow the car as Ed slowed to wave, and his sluggish steps seemed strangely out of sync with his youthful frame. One morning, Ed stopped at the farm house and inquired.

The colt's name was Carlson. His owner, challenged with a medical condition, could do little more than see to the animal's basic needs. "Would you be willing to sell?" Ed asked. And on the following weekend, Ed was on his way to pick up Carlson and take him to his new home.

Within a month, Carlson's soft brown eyes were shining with interest and intelligence. His movements quickened, and his playful prance made Ed's heart swell with pride. "Carlson," he said, "all you needed was a little love, and you're a whole new creature!"

Beyond the Basics

Just as the body needs nourishment to remain healthy and strong, so does the spirit. Our inner growth begins when God's Spirit enters our heart, enabling us to see beyond the many physical things clamoring for our attention. We develop and mature within as we come to realize that there's more to life than simply physical needs and desires, such as food and water, shelter and material possessions. There's also God.

Our attention to things of the spirit turns us into new creatures. We admit that possessions don't satisfy us, and money and status aren't as fulfilling as we once thought. We grow in wisdom about eternal things, because we're able to look beyond the present moment. We develop love and compassion for others as we realize that we ourselves need God's love and compassion. We're able to play, laugh, and enjoy life in a way not possible without a vibrant, healthy spirit within us.

Life is more than the basics. We were created for more—much more!

Dear God, send Your Spirit into my heart so I may live life to the fullest. Amen

Care, and not fine stables,
makes a good horse.
Danish proverb

Are we not all divine?
Are we not all made for a higher life?
Mother Teresa

Behold, I make all things new.
Revelation 21:5

The man who has no inner life
is a slave of his surroundings,
as the barometer is the obedient
servant of the air at rest.
Henri F. Amiel

You have as much laughter
as you have faith.
Martin Luther

All I have seen teaches me to trust the
Creator for all I have not seen.
Ralph Waldo Emerson

If any man be in Christ,
he is a new creature:
old things are passed away; behold,
all things are become new.
2 Corinthians 5:17

Her happy nicker is sunshine to my
heart and her playful gambol tickles
the child in me...a horse's appreciation
of life's simple blessings lifts my heart
in gratitude for all creation.
T. J. Highland

Spirituality is the process
of getting our minds off ourselves
and back on God.
Author unknown

The west-winds blow, and, singing low,
I hear the glad streams run;
The windows of my soul I throw
Wide open to the sun.
John Greenleaf Whittier

Beneath a clear autumn sky, horse and rider sweep as one free spirit across the verdant meadow. With only a flick of the reins and click of the tongue, the rider points her mount toward the low wooden hurdle, and the animal leaps with agility and grace. With equal ease, she guides her lively steed in a wide circle, over the hurdle once again, and finally back to the familiar pasture of home.

The rider alights bathed in smiles, and her horse whinnies and nods with pleasure. They know each other well, and they luxuriate in each other's company. Both in their own way lavish on each other affection, loyalty, and companionship.

After all, they're friends, and that's what friends are for.

Friends Forever

There are people we like right from the first hello. Somehow we feel we've known them for a long time, and when we get talking, we discover we share a lot in common. It's a mutual attraction that grows into a deep and lasting friendship.

In a similar way, God's love for you has attracted Him to you. He invites you to let Him lead you closer to Him, and He's eager to hear your response. When you talk to Him about your cares and concerns, your hopes and dreams, He takes pleasure in your sharing, your openness, your honesty. And it's not a one-sided conversation. He is present to soothe your anxieties, renew your soul, and open your heart and mind to His guidance in your life.

The relationship God offers to you is not just for a moment in time, or even for a lifetime. It's a relationship designed by God to last forever.

Dear God, thank You for inviting me to follow You and know You as my provider, protector, and friend. Amen

*He brought me forth also
into a large place; he delivered me,
because he delighted in me.*
Psalm 18:19

Friendship is a sheltering tree.
Samuel Taylor Coleridge

*The LORD is nigh unto all them that
call upon him, to all that call
upon him in truth.*
Psalm 145:18

**We learn that God is,
that He is in me, and that all things
are shadows of Him.**
Ralph Waldo Emerson

*A friend is one who knows you as
you are, understands where you've
been, accepts who you've become,
and still gently invites you to grow.*
Author unknown

**I heard a neigh. Oh, such a brisk and
melodious neigh as that was!
My very heart leaped with delight
at the sound.**
Nathaniel Hawthorne

*The most I can do for my friend
is simply be his friend.*
Henry David Thoreau

**There is no possession more valuable
than a good and faithful friend.**
Socrates

Every Saturday morning, Deb rode her beloved palomino, Angel, through trails that wound from the back of the stable and through adjoining woods and fields. It was her time for quiet, a time she put behind her the week's worries and responsibilities, projects and deadlines. During their time together, Angel listened patiently when Deb wanted to talk and proved a quiet companion when she just needed to think. The steady rhythm of her hooves on the path relaxed Deb, and it was during these hours that she felt closest to herself, to nature, and to God.

To Deb, Angel was a true angel, and she couldn't imagine life without her. Back at the stable, Deb would hand her a treat as she stroked her creamy muzzle. Without a doubt, Angel understood how much she meant to her owner and companion.

A Shady Trail

Quiet time is essential to our physical, mental, and spiritual well-being. How well we know it, yet with today's constant buzz of activity and insistence on 24/7 connectedness, we often put quiet time aside until "later." More days pass, and "later" never comes.

A Sabbath—a time of rest—is a traditional practice well worth preserving. In ancient days, people would stop work altogether and gather for worship, celebration, and family time. As they rested from work, so did the animals that helped them plow the fields and pull their carts. It was a time of renewal for all God's creatures.

Your own time of rest begins with your decision to clear a place in your calendar for recreation, meditation, and prayer. It asks for you to make quiet time a priority, not an option. Why? You already know: rest is something easily put off until "later." You already know that there's no better time than now to get in touch with yourself, with nature, and with God.

Dear God, help me commit to keeping a regular time of spiritual rest and renewal. Amen

*The best thing must be
to flee from all to the All.*
Teresa of Avila

**Today if ye will hear his voice,
harden not your heart.**
Psalm 95:7-8

*Rest is not idleness, and to lie
sometimes on the grass under the
trees on a summer's day, listening
to the murmur of water, or watching
the clouds float across the sky,
is by no means a waste of time.*
John Lubbock

**Riding a horse is not a gentle hobby,
to be picked up and laid
down like a game of Solitaire.
It is a grand passion.**
Ralph Waldo Emerson

*Nothing gives rest but the sincere
search for truth.*
Blaise Pascal

**Remember the sabbath day,
to keep it holy.**
Exodus 20:8

*Take rest; a field that has rested
gives a bountiful crop.*
Ovid

**I bless the hoss from hoof to head —
From head to hoof, and tale to mane! —
I bless the hoss, as I have said,
From head to hoof, and back again!**
James Whitcomb Riley

*I need nothing but God, and to lose
myself in the heart of God.*
Margaret Mary Alacoque

From tender foal attempting to stand on her
long, wobbly legs, to grand dame of pasture
and field, a horse is one of nature's wonders.
Just watching the antics of colts and fillies frol-
icking in the corral never fails to bring a smile.
That's honest to goodness horseplay!

Those who know the art of teaching a young
horse to trot and gallop, to prance and parade
know the rewards of nurturing the talents,
abilities, and intelligence of another living creature. Those who shelter and befriend, admire
and love, enjoy and appreciate horses find in
them a faithful and affectionate companion.

In later years of her cherished life the aged
horse is drawn toward familiar pastures, enjoy-
ing the simple pleasures of sweet grass and
a warm sun. She has seen many days, heard
many voices, knows many things…her wisdom
whispers in the depth of her soft brown eyes.

Seasonal Gifts

From the wonder of childhood to the wisdom of age, each season of life holds its own miracles. At the passing of one stage, another unfolds, and with it brings things to learn, discoveries to make, and experiences to embrace and enjoy.

But just as in nature's seasons, each life-season has its challenges. There's the inexperience of youth and the physical weakness of old age...the responsibilities of adulthood and the sorrow of loss. It's when we focus only on these things, however, that we lose sight of the miracles and the blessings all around us.

No matter where you are in life, there are new pathways for you to explore. There are things for you to do now that you were never able to do before, and you have knowledge and understanding today that you didn't have yesterday.

Let the power of your imagination take you on a "ride" through the wonders great and small surrounding you this day!

> **Thank You, God, for all the days of my life you have given me to embrace, explore, and enjoy. Amen**

Let me tell thee,
time is a very precious gift of God;
so precious that it's only given to us
moment by moment.
Amelia Barr

Jesus said, Suffer little children,
and forbid them not, to come unto me:
for of such is the kingdom of heaven.
Matthew 19:14

May you live all the days of your life.
Jonathan Swift

Know the true value of time; snatch,
seize, and enjoy every moment of it.
No idleness, no laziness,
no procrastination: never put off till
tomorrow what you can do today.
Lord Chesterfield

Teach us to number our days,
that we may apply our hearts
unto wisdom.
Psalm 90:12

An inborn love of the horse is instinctive, quite unreasoning, and one cannot recall any beginning of what seems to have always been there, together with a craving for perfection in the object of interest.
Lady Ann Blunt

Even to your old age and gray hairs I am he, I am he who will sustain you. I have made you and I will carry you; I will sustain you and I will rescue you.
Isaiah 46:4 NIV

Happiness is produced not so much by great pieces of good fortune that seldom happen, as by little advantages that occur every day.
Benjamin Franklin

When I am anxious, it is because I am living in the future. When I am depressed, it is because I am living in the past. When I am fulfilled, I am living in the present.
Author unknown

That summer, George decided he would ride her. She was an awesome coppery-red chestnut show horse, and she had spark and energy to burn. When George went to mount her, she jostled and jiggled, shook and squirmed. The next thing he knew, he was clutching the saddle and hanging with one leg in the stirrup and the other on the ground as she whirled around in circles. The best he could do, he figured, was hang on and wait for her to settle down.

Just then the horse trainer showed up. "Waitin' for her to settle down," George yelled in explanation. It was then George heard advice he never forgot. "If you wait until everything's just right," the trainer said, "you'll never get anything done. Now get up in the saddle and ride!"

And he did.

Saddle Up

No matter how long we wait, that "perfect time" never comes. There's always something to hold us back, and often, what's holding us back is our own reluctance to do what we say we're yearning to do. Perhaps we want to protect ourselves from failure, or we're not willing to give our dream the effort it would take to make it real.

If the "perfect time" is the only thing standing between you and what you want to achieve, why not talk it over with God? In quiet prayer and meditation, you can get past imaginary hindrances and discern His will for you. By talking it over with mature friends and advisors, you may realize that there's nothing blocking you except your firm commitment.

Why simply hang on? It may not be the perfect time, but perhaps it's the right time to "get up in the saddle and ride!"

Dear God, grant me the power to do those God-pleasing things that You have put in my heart to do. Amen

And whatsoever ye do,
do it heartily, as to the Lord,
and not unto men.
Colossians 3:23

Have a purpose in life, and having it,
throw into your work
such strength of mind and muscle as
God has given you.
Thomas Carlyle

About the head of a truly great
horse there is an air of freedom
unconquerable. The eyes seem to
look on heights beyond our gaze.
It is the look of a spirit that can soar.
John Taintor Foote

From a shy, timid girl I had become a
woman of resolute character,
who could no longer be frightened by
the struggle with troubles.
Anna Dostoevsky

I am not bound to win, but I am
bound to be true. I am not bound to
succeed, but I am bound to live up
to what light I have.
Abraham Lincoln

When a man does not know what
harbor he is heading for,
no wind is the right wind.
Seneca

Whether therefore ye eat,
or drink, or whatsoever ye do,
do all to the glory of God.
1 Corinthians 10:31

What one has, one ought to use;
and whatever he does, he should do
with all his might.
Cicero

To ride a horse is to ride the sky.
Author unknown

Vigor is contagious,
and whatever makes us either think
or feel strongly adds to our power
and enlarges our field of action.
Ralph Waldo Emerson

He that waits upon fortune is never
sure of a dinner.
Benjamin Franklin

Never grow a wishbone, daughter,
where a backbone ought to be.
Clementine Paddleford

Remember, people will judge you
by your actions, not your intentions.
You may have a heart of gold, but so
does a hard-boiled egg.
Author unknown

Do what you can, with what you
have, where you are.
Theodore Roosevelt

Do not wait for ideal circumstances,
nor for the best opportunities;
they will never come.
Janet Erskine Stuart

*Opportunity is missed by most
people because it is dressed in
overalls and looks like work.*
Thomas Alva Edison

Nothing ventured, nothing gained.
Saying

*You can imagine yourself astride
a spirited horse...or you can
get in the saddle and experience
the adventure.*
T. J. Highland

**As we have therefore opportunity,
let us do good unto all men,
especially unto them who are
of the household of faith.**
Galatians 6:10

*Lose yourself wholly; and the more
you lose, the more you will find.*
Catherine of Siena

Destiny possessed a rare combination
of pure strength and natural gentleness.
His large muscular body exuded power,
and he cut an intimidating figure as he
grazed out in the pasture. Most people
felt wary about approaching him, but once
mounted, the horse's true spirit came out.
He was the calmest, kindest creature in
the world.

Straddling Destiny, riders felt secure in his
strength and relied on his sure-footedness
over rough terrain. Riders who trusted
Destiny rather than attempt to exert
control over him rested at ease in the
benevolence of his gentle nature.

Destiny was like a man secure in his own
strength. He embraces kindness, tender-
ness, and goodwill because he has nothing
to prove to anyone.

Beyond Description

What picture comes to mind when you think about God? Does He look like a mighty king or a tender Father? As it happens, God is both these things—and more!

God possesses power beyond our understanding, and that's why we can lean on Him to take care of those things far outside our ability—things like our inner peace, our spiritual wholeness, and our eternal life. He has the ability and willingness to carry us beyond our fears and anxieties, and bring us safely home.

He also possesses compassion beyond our imagination. He yearns to forgive and make new, to cleanse and refresh the humble heart. His whole desire is to embrace us in His never-ending love and show us the joy of believing in Him.

As we come to know Him better, we realize no one picture, no one word, could possibly encompass Him. He is our indescribable God!

**Bring me to know You better, dear God,
as I travel through the days and years of my life.
Amen**

Great is our Lord, and of great
power: his understanding is infinite.
Psalm 147:5

If you say that God is good, great,
blessed, wise or any such thing, the
starting point is this: God is.
Bernard of Clairvaux

There is no object that we see; no
action that we do; no good that we
enjoy; no evil that we feel, or fear,
but we may make some spiritual
advantage of all: and he that makes
such improvement is wise,
as well as pious.
Anne Bradstreet

Some people want to see God with
their eyes as they see a cow, and to
love Him as they love their cow—for
the milk and cheese and profit it brings
them. This is how it is with people who
love God for the sake of outward
wealth or inward comfort.
Meister Eckhart

God is concealed from the mind
but revealed in the heart.
Author unknown

You, O Lord, are a compassionate
and gracious God, slow to anger,
abounding in love and faithfulness.
Psalm 86:15 NIV

In the wonders of creation,
I see His creativity,
His magnificence, His might.
T. J. Highland

God is to me that creative Force,
behind and in the universe,
who manifests Himself as energy,
as life, as order, as beauty, as thought,
as conscience, as love.
Henry Sloane Coffin

When a horse suffers an injury due to
a fall, prompt and proficient veterinary
care can often save broken limbs and
repair splintered bones. Yet there's more
to healing than a cast, splint, or bandage.
There's something the best medicines can't
give, and that's the comfort of knowing
someone cares. The sound of a familiar
voice, the reassurance of a gentle touch,
the sight of a beloved face can make all
the difference.

Miracle stories of regained health—both of
horses and of humans—stem from a firm
belief in the innate value of life and the
willingness of others to support and encourage those who suffer. As skillful hands
can mend a wound, tender hearts can
soothe the sorrow until new life awakens.

From the darkness of night, a new day
dawns. That's the time of new beginnings
for all God's creatures.

A New Beginning

A major medical event or natural catastrophe can leave us with a whole new outlook on life. No longer are we prone to complain about minor annoyances after we have narrowly escaped disaster. No more will we let another day go by without taking time to marvel at the beauty of sunshine, the colors of a rainbow, the miracle of growth.

Your spiritual new beginning happens the moment you turn to God's Spirit for healing. Whether it's for the first time or for the hundredth time you have come to Him, your great physician of the soul reaches out with the balm of His comfort and presence, His compassion and forgiveness. His answer to hearts broken by disappointment or hopelessness, physical illness or spiritual anguish, is unconditional love.

Without fail, God's healing hand leads you from endings to beginnings...from despair to victory.

Dear God, let your life-giving Spirit enter my heart so I may find wholeness of body and soul. Amen

*To live is so startling it leaves little
time for anything else.*
Emily Dickinson

**The real voyage of discovery consists
not in seeking new landscapes but in
having new eyes.**
Marcel Proust

*Every new beginning comes from
some other beginning's end.*
Seneca

**Come unto me, all ye that labour
and are heavy laden,
and I will give you rest.**
Matthew 11:28

*Man's mind stretched to a new
idea never goes back to its
original dimensions.*
Oliver Wendell Holmes

**We must always change, renew,
rejuvenate ourselves;
otherwise we harden.**
Johann Wolfgang von Goethe

When I first open my eyes upon
the morning meadows and look out
upon the beautiful world,
I thank God I am alive.
Ralph Waldo Emerson

He healeth the broken in heart,
and bindeth up their wounds.
Psalm 147:3

One appreciates that daily life is
really good when one wakes from a
horrible dream, or when one takes
the first outing after a sickness.
Why not realize it now?
William Lyon Phelps

Be glad of life because it gives you the
chance to love, and to work, and to
play and to look up at the stars.
Henry van Dyke

There are some defeats more
triumphant than victories.
Michel de Montaigne

To everyone, she was an unlikely candidate to win a prize at our state fair, but not to Jill. To her, the awkward colt had spit and spirit, and Jill knew that he could be a real champion if he wanted to be.

All summer Jill worked with him, leading him through trots and canters. She rewarded him with apples and carrots every time he did what she wanted him to do. Gradually, the colt started to take on the exercises with enthusiasm, as if Jill's goal was now his goal. All the energy he used to waste in aimless romping, he now channeled into perfectly executed steps and prances. He was proud of himself, and so was Jill.

Jill prizes the ribbon he won at the fair. And after that, no one doubted Jill when she pointed to a colt and said, "That one has a lot of promise."

An Eye for Beauty

A person's physical appearance is the first thing we see. When we reach a conclusion about that person based on appearance, however, we're more than likely wrong. We're seeing only the outside, but the inside—the heart—is invisible to us. Only God can read the heart.

God fully knows our weaknesses and strengths, our motivations and values. He desires to see within us Spirit-planted seeds of love, compassion, and caring, and He knows that each of us has the ability to make our world a better place. But are these good seeds being nourished and cared for? Are they flourishing?

To God's eyes, the appearance of your heart matters more—much more—than the appearance of your body, because from your heart lasting beauty grows. With Spirit-led guidance, His seeds of holiness flower into real, visible, earth-changing and world-blessing acts of love. He sees it in your heart, because He has put it there.

Dear God, thank You for blessing me with spiritual beauty. Lead and guide me so I can live up to my true potential. Amen

The LORD seeth not as man seeth;
for man looketh on the outward
appearance, but the LORD
looketh on the heart.
1 Samuel 16:7

Goodness coming from the heart
quietly blesses every other heart.
Author unknown

The splendor of a horse rests less
in the appearance of his coat, and
more in the fire within his heart.
T. J. Highland

A kind heart is a fountain of gladness,
making everything in its
vicinity freshen into smiles.
Washington Irving

Things do not pass for what they
are, but for what they seem. Most
things are judged by their jackets.
Baltasar Gracian

If I can stop one heart from breaking,
I shall not live in vain;
If I can ease one life the aching,
Or cool one pain,
Or help one fainting robin
Unto his nest again,
I shall not live in vain.

Emily Dickinson

Many children, entranced by the elegance and agility of horses, picture themselves astride one of the spirited animals. What fun! What freedom to ride with the wind! Little do they realize how much they need to learn before they're ready to take a horse out on their own.

Their first riding lessons will not find them galloping across wide-open pastures, but learning how to mount and dismount, how to hold the reins, and how to communicate with the horse. An instructor will teach them how to sit comfortably and confidently so the animal will accept their presence and obey their directions.

Children who learn the skills they need and are willing to practice are those who, in a short time, are sitting astride a horse many times their size with assurance and style. They're the lucky kids who inspire the next generation of young horse-lovers who can't wait to revel in the freedom of the wind!

Stable Training

God never expects us to naturally know how to live a spiritual life. That's why He puts people in our life to "train" us through their advice, conversation, example, and encouragement. He sends His Spirit into our hearts to fill us with God-pleasing desires, and He reveals in the Bible His commandments, His purpose for our life, and His plan for our future.

As with most things we're in the process of learning, we make mistakes. Sometimes it's because we're not listening to our guide, and sometimes it's because we need more practice before the good thoughts, words, and actions we want become easy and natural. In either case, God is forgiving and patient and willing to show us again how to do things His way.

With Him as your trainer, you learn how to live life from the one who has blessed you with life.

Guide me, dear God, so I may experience the pleasure and delight of knowing and doing Your will. Amen

Thou shalt guide me with thy
counsel, and afterward
receive me to glory.
Psalm 73:24

A teacher affects eternity; he can
never tell where his influence stops.
Henry Brooks Adams

To tend, unfailingly, unflinchingly,
towards a goal,
is the secret of success.
Anna Pavlova

The strength of a man consists in
finding out the way in which God is
going, and going in that way, too.
Henry Ward Beecher

God does not will that we abound
in knowledge, but that we lovingly
and humbly submit ourselves in all
things to His will.
Henry Suso

*Our chief want in life is somebody
who shall make us what we can be.*
Ralph Waldo Emerson

**Show me your ways, LORD,
teach me your paths. Guide me in
your truth and teach me,
for you are God my Savior.**
Psalm 25:4-5 NIV

*People seldom improve when they
have no model but themselves
to copy after.*
Oliver Goldsmith

**Keep away from people who try to
belittle your ambitions. Small people
always do that, but the really great
make you feel that you, too,
can become great.**
Mark Twain

*Excellence encourages one about
life generally; it shows the spiritual
wealth of the world.*
George Eliot

During John's freshman year in college, he spent Christmas break with his roommate and his family. They lived on a farm, and they invited John to ride their chestnut mare, Glory, whenever he wanted.

Late one afternoon when his roommate was out, John decided to ride Glory into town. He followed the trail his roommate had pointed out earlier, and then he explored nearby paths.

By the time he started back, evening had enveloped the woods in darkness. About midway through, he realized he was lost. He pulled the reins in the direction he thought he should go, but Glory neighed and veered in the opposite direction. John pulled again, and the horse veered again. In desperation, he stopped struggling and let Glory lead.

Relief flooded over him as he emerged from the trail and spied the lights shining from the windows of the family's farmhouse. He gave Glory a grateful pat as she headed straight to her corral.

Horse Sense

When we're searching for spiritual truth, it can be like trying to find our way in the dark. We head in one direction only to find the path isn't taking us where we want to go; then start in another direction not knowing whether we're heading toward wisdom or disappointment.

The best path to follow when you're in spiritual darkness is the one God's Son Jesus has laid out. He knows the way to God because He has made the journey from heaven to earth and back again. As the living God, Jesus is willing and able to lead you through the darkness of uncertainty and into the radiance of His love. He is the way, the truth, and the light.

Who better to trust for directions than the person who has already been there? That's why Jesus came into the world and why He invites you to stop struggling and let Him lead you safely home.

Dear God, pour Your Spirit into my heart so I may know the direction to go. Amen

I am come a light into the world,
that whosoever believeth on me
should not abide in darkness.
John 12:46

Nothing gives rest but the sincere
search for truth.
Blaise Pascal

The great blessings of mankind are
within us, and within our reach; but
we shut our eyes and, like people in
the dark, fall short of the very thing
we search for without finding it.
Seneca

There is an inmost center in us all,
where truth abides in fullness.
Robert Browning

Truly, it is in darkness that one finds
the light, so when we are in sorrow,
then this light is nearest of all to us.
Meister Eckhart

Turn your face to the sun and the
shadows fall behind you.
Maori proverb

Thy word is a lamp unto my feet,
and a light unto my path.
Psalm 119:105

[Jesus said,] "I am the light of the
world. Whoever follows me will
never walk in darkness,
but will have the light of life."
John 8:12 NIV

Beyond a doubt truth bears
the same relation to falsehood
as light to darkness.
Leonardo da Vinci

A man should learn to detect and
watch that gleam of light which
flashes across his mind from within.
Ralph Waldo Emerson

Horses, like people, aren't meant to be alone. In nature, they're herd animals, and they crave companionship and relish the presence of others, be they humans, horses, or other creatures.

It's not uncommon for a horse to bond with the rooster that shares her barn, or the kitten that clambers atop her as she feeds from her bag of oats. Horses have been known to kick and neigh in protest if they are led away from the goat that nuzzles up to them at bedtime, or if they're missing the puppy that always scampers around their pasture during the day.

A horse and a kitten? A mare and a goat? There's no difference in color, shape, or size when two hearts share the precious bond of friendship.

A Good Herd

Though God created us as unique individuals, we were made for one another. Not one of us is truly self-sufficient, but rather dependent on others—sometimes for physical care, but always for emotional support and practical advice, and for sincere praise and spiritual support.

The people around us supply the gifts and talents we may lack, just as we in turn enrich their world with what we're skilled at doing. The words we say have the power to lighten a heavy spirit, build up a flagging will, and soothe a weary soul. Our prayers for one another please God, for He delights in hearts that care.

God is always present, and He enables us to be there for others, and for others to be there for us. We were never meant to live in isolation, but connected to one another through the bonds of family, friendship, community, and common humanity.

Dear God, send Your Spirit into my heart that I may reach out to others with generosity and kindness, and receive the blessing of others in return. Amen

Let us not give up meeting together,
as some are in the habit of doing,
but let us encourage one another.
Hebrews 10:25 NIV

In every union there is a mystery.
Henri F. Amiel

The day I saw the rooster sitting
contentedly on the back of our pony
I realized that friendship comes in
all shapes and sizes.
T. J. Highland

My friends are my estate.
Emily Dickinson

The most empowering relationships
are those in which each partner lifts
the other to a higher possession of
their own being.
Teilhard de Chardin

When I give, I give myself.
Walt Whitman

**Loneliness is the
most terrible poverty.**
Mother Teresa

*If we walk in the light, as he is in the
light, we have fellowship
one with another.*
1 John 1:7

**A cheer, then, for the noblest breast
That fears not danger's post;
And like the lifeboat, proves a friend,
When friends are wanted most.**
Eliza Cook

*There is something special and good
in each of us. Cultivate it in yourself–
Encourage it in others.*
Author Unknown

The jittery colt had been through a lot by the time he came to us, so we did everything we could to make his new home comfortable and quiet. We visited him throughout the day, offering him juicy apples and fresh, fragrant carrots to tempt his appetite as we spoke to him in hushed tones. Sometimes we simply sat in the barn with him and let him watch us with his timid, wary eyes.

Within a few months, the colt we named Maxwell started responding to our attentions. He began to come forward when we held out his treats and to let us stroke his silky mane. Gradually he gained weight, filled out, and grew in strength and confidence. He learned to trust again.

Our beloved Maxwell holds a special place in our hearts, because he taught us the profound power of care and compassion, kindness and love.

A Matter of Trust

If you have ever taught a timid animal to come to you, you know the joy of watching frightened eyes turn soft and trusting. Little by little, its anxiety lessens and the creature welcomes your approach, lifting its head for a stroke of your hand and responding with grateful pleasure. What a heartwarming reward for your compassion, patience, and love!

If you are reluctant to trust your heavenly Father in all ways, picture yourself as that creature. Then picture God listening patiently as you speak to Him about those things that cause you doubt, hesitation, and uncertainty. Watch Him surround you with His presence and nourish you with His forgiveness and compassion. This is His way of showering you with peace and comfort. This is how He heals you so you can trust again.

God desires your trust, and He will work to get it. Every day, He will be there for you. Little by little, your trust increases...your faith grows...your joy unfolds.

Dear God, please begin this day to lead me closer to You. Amen

[Love] always protects, always
trusts, always hopes,
always perseveres.
1 Corinthians 13:7 NIV

Doubt of whatever kind,
can be ended by Action alone.
Thomas Carlyle

The LORD is my strength and my
shield; my heart trusted in him, and
I am helped: therefore my heart
greatly rejoiceth; and with my song
will I praise him.
Psalm 28:7

To be what we are, and to become
what we are capable of becoming,
is the only end of life.
Robert Louis Stevenson

Few delights can equal the mere
presence of one whom we
trust utterly.
George MacDonald

As soon as you trust yourself,
you will know how to live.
Johann Wolfgang von Goethe

**He that takes truth for his guide, and
duty for his end, may safely trust to
God's providence to lead him aright.**
Blaise Pascal

I think we may safely trust a good
deal more than we do.
Henry David Thoreau

**Commit thy way unto the LORD; trust
also in him; and he shall bring it to pass.
And he shall bring forth thy
righteousness as the light,
and thy judgment as the noonday.**
Psalm 37:5-6

As long as Gail could remember, there was Dimples, a small brown pony that lived in the barn outside. As soon as she could talk, she'd beg her mother to take her outside so they could visit.

One rainy day when Gail was four, she decided Dimples must be cold and lonely out there in the barn. Without telling anyone, she opened the back door, carefully walked down the steps and across to the barn. "Come on, Dimples," she said. "You can come into my room where it's warm and we can play."

The clomp of hooves across the kitchen floor startled her mother, who came running downstairs. When she saw child and horse, she stopped, and calmly walked over to Dimples. She softly talked to her as she led the horse back outside and into her stall. When she returned, she talked to her soft-hearted daughter about the different needs of ponies and people.

Beyond Imagining

It's easy to forget that God is God! He possesses thoughts far beyond our limited reasoning, and His authority extends throughout space and time. His power and might, wisdom and knowledge we can't possibly imagine.

Yet we're tempted to measure God by our own abilities—perhaps magnified, but still bound by human ideas and concepts. When we do, we short-change Him, and we short-change ourselves. We miss out on appreciating the miracles and marvels He puts before us every day, and we fail to receive great things from Him because we doubt His ability to grant them.

In our almighty God, we have a source of help, comfort, and wisdom far outside our own experience and power. We have someone to talk to, to pray to, and to ask whatever we need according to His will—even if we think we're asking for the impossible.

God is your all-powerful creator, and you are His beloved creation. Let God be God to you!

Let me rely on You, dear God, because you are my God. Amen

[Faith] looks upward and decries
objects remote; but reason can
discover things only near, and sees
nothing that is above her.
Francis Quarles

With God nothing shall be impossible.
Luke 1:37

God's gifts put man's
best dreams to shame.
Elizabeth Barrett Browning

It is the heart which experiences God, and not the reason. This, then, is faith: God felt by the heart, not by the reason.
Blaise Pascal

God is a circle whose center
is everywhere,
and its circumference nowhere.
Empedocles

Until now you have not asked for
anything in my name.
Ask and you will receive,
and your joy will be complete.
John 16:24 NIV

**God is that infinite All of which man
knows himself to be a finite part.**
Leo Tolstoy

All are but parts
of one stupendous whole,
Whose body Nature is,
and God the soul.
Alexander Pope

**We are but a point, a single comma,
and God is the literature of eternity.**
Henry Ward Beecher

The rider, a slight girl no more than ten years old, sat astride the massive gelding with ease. She maneuvered him through his exercises with seeming effortlessness, using subtle movements of her hands on the reins to direct the animal around markers and over hurdles. The bit in the horse's mouth communicated her directions.

When she started lessons, she was shocked to learn that a bit, a metal device, is used to control a horse. "But doesn't it hurt?" she cried to her trainer. "No," the woman explained, "not if the right bit is inserted with care and used the right way."

The girl learned about different kinds of bits, how to put a bit in the horse's mouth, and the correct way to hold the reins so the bit can be worn comfortably by the horse and used productively by the rider.

A Bit in the Mouth

There's nothing like a real verbal blunder to remind us of the power of a single word! Indeed, the words that come out of our mouth can hurt, embarrass, offend, and deceive; they can cause pain, misinform, and hide the truth. But that's only half of it.

Words can comfort broken hearts, strengthen weak relationships, and build bridges between people. Words used wisely and well have the power to inform and enlighten, educate and teach. With words we communicate with ourselves, with others, and with God—and the words we choose matter.

Our outlook on life, as well as our relationship with others and with God, depends largely on the words we use in thought and in speech. Truthful, affirming, and positive words bless our lives and the lives of those we touch. They nurture heart and mind. They become our strength and our freedom when we learn how to control them and choose them with care.

Dear God, let my words be a source of goodness for me and for everyone whose life I touch. Amen

Behold, we put bits in the horses'
mouths, that they may obey us; and
we turn about their whole body.
James 3:3

Blessed is the man who,
having nothing to say, abstains from
giving wordy evidence of the fact.
George Eliot

Once a word has been allowed to
escape, it cannot be recalled.
Horace

To talk without thinking
is to shoot without aiming.
English proverb

To speak and to speak well
are two things. A fool may talk,
but a wise man speaks.
Ben Jonson

One of the things that keep us at a
distance from perfection is, without
doubt, our tongue.
Francis de Sales

The true genius shudders at
incompleteness—and usually prefers
silence to saying something which is
not everything it should be.
Edgar Allan Poe

Speak when you are angry
and you will make the best speech
you will ever regret.
Ambrose Bierce

Words are not as satisfactory as we
should like them to be, but, like our
neighbors, we have got to live with
them and must make the best and not
the worst of them.
Samuel Butler

Let your speech be always with grace,
seasoned with salt, that ye may know
how ye ought to answer every man.
Colossians 4:6

Discretion in speech
is more than eloquence.
Francis Bacon

*A word fitly spoken is like apples of
gold in pictures of silver.*
Proverbs 25:11

**A statement once let loose cannot be
caught by four horses.**
Japanese proverb

*We have too many high sounding
words, and too few actions that
correspond with them.*
Abigail Adams

**Violence of the tongue is very real—
sharper than any knife.**
Mother Teresa

*Words should be scattered like
seed: no matter how small the seed
may be, if it has once found
favorable ground,
it unfolds its strength.*
Seneca

The right word may be effective,
but no word was ever as effective
as a rightly timed pause.
Mark Twain

Kind words produce their
own image in men's souls;
and what a beautiful image it is.
Blaise Pascal

O Lord, open my lips, and my mouth
will declare your praise.
Psalm 51:15 NIV

Watch your thoughts,
they become words.
Watch your words,
they become actions.
Watch your actions,
they become habits.
Watch your habits,
they become your character.
Watch your character,
it becomes your destiny.
Author unknown

Why couldn't I have a pony? Our back yard was big enough, and we had a shed that could be made into a barn. Dad could mend the fence, I said to Mom, and my pony wouldn't bother anyone. I told Mom how much a pony cost, and I knew she and Dad could afford it.

That's when Mom sat me down for a chat. "It's not simply the price of the horse," she explained, "but the cost of food, supplies, and veterinary care. There's also work—a lot of work! Do you want to get up an hour earlier every morning to feed and water your pony?" She smiled, because she knew mornings were hard for me. "And then come straight home from school every afternoon to exercise and groom your pony...and muck out the stall?"

Yes, there was a lot more to keeping a pony than I had ever thought!

A Daily Commitment

Many people start out on the spiritual path with enthusiasm, but their interest fades with time. Perhaps they miss the thrill of discovering spiritual concepts and the excitement of making new friends in a worship community. Often they emerge disappointed that the warmth and closeness of God's presence isn't as apparent to their senses as it was in the beginning.

There's more to a true spiritual journey than an initial flood of words and feelings. Rather, it's an all-day, every-day commitment with low and high points, difficult and easy moments, inspiring and lackluster times. Only our Spirit-inspired commitment to God and our own spiritual growth keeps us on His path, and we're rewarded with increased understanding, wisdom, and peace.

God desires to draw you closer to Him. He does this as you take time to meditate and pray. He does this as you think about Him and His work in your life. He does this because He's fully committed to you.

Thank You, dear God, for your commitment to me. Grant me the power to commit myself to You! Amen

*Thou shalt love the LORD thy God
with all thine heart, and with all thy
soul, and with all thy might.*

Deuteronomy 6:5

**That which we persist in doing
becomes easier—not that the nature
of the task has changed,
but our ability to do it has increased.**

Ralph Waldo Emerson

*Let us hold fast the profession
of our faith without wavering;
(for he is faithful that promised).*

Hebrews 10:23

**Now I am steel-set:
I follow the call to the clear radiance
and glow of the heights.**

Henrik Ibsen

*Let my name stand among those
who are willing to bear ridicule and
reproach for the truth's sake,
and so earn some right to rejoice
when the victory is won.*

Louisa May Alcott

I am seeking, I am striving,
I am in it with all my heart.
Vincent van Gogh

Let us not be weary in well doing:
for in due season we shall reap,
if we faint not.
Galatians 6:9

I know of no more
encouraging fact than the
unquestionable ability of man to
elevate his life by conscious endeavor.
Henry David Thoreau

The victory of success is half done
when one gains the habit of work.
Sarah Knowles Bolton

When you have decided what you
believe, and what you feel must be
done, have the courage to stand alone
and be counted.
Eleanor Roosevelt

While some owners start training their racing colts and fillies early, others believe in waiting until the animals have reached their fourth year. A friend of mine was of this persuasion. "The extra year gives the horse's body a chance to grow stronger, so there's less chance of injury," he said. "The horse is more mature, and strong enough to go through the exercises his training requires. When he's ready for racing, he's mentally and physically ready to compete on the track."

Sure, this trainer loses the winnings a younger race horse might bring in. His patience pays off, however, in the many years of good health his race horses enjoy and in the thrill of healthy competition.

Training Grounds

Spirituality doesn't come instantly. There's no switch to flip and it's suddenly there, and there's no button to click and it's delivered to you the next day. Instead, spirituality is a lifelong process of beginning, growing, and maturing...of prayer and practice, of thought and action, of being and doing.

God guides you to deeper understanding when He sees you're ready, and He permits tests and challenges to your faith when He knows you have what it takes to overcome them. God has a plan and a purpose for you, but, in His wisdom, He also has a timetable. It may not be the same as someone else's; you need never fret if the next person seems so much more spiritually advanced than you are.

God knows exactly the right times for you to study and learn, to follow and teach, to speak and listen. And unlike most kinds of training, spiritual training is a lifelong process, pleasure, and, most of all, a privilege!

**Teach me, dear God, to trust Your wisdom,
Your guidance, and Your timetable. Amen**

True worth is doing each day some little good, not dreaming of great things to do by and by.
Author unknown

A thousand years in thy sight are but as yesterday when it is past, and as a watch in the night.
Psalm 90:4

Most people would succeed in small things if they were not troubled with great ambitions.
Henry Wadsworth Longfellow

A good horse makes short miles.
George Eliot

To every thing there is a season, and a time to every purpose under the heaven.
Ecclesiastes 3:1

Not to go back is somewhat to advance. And men must walk, at least, before they dance.
Alexander Pope

Little drops of water,
little grains of sand,
Make the mighty ocean,
and the pleasant land:
So the little minutes,
humble though they be,
Make the mighty ages
of eternity.
Little deeds of kindness,
little words of love,
Help to make earth happy,
like Heaven up above.

Julia Carney

Every year Don and Alice took their three
children to the horse show. Alice loved
to see their faces fill with wonder as they
watched the magnificent animals prance in
perfect formation around the arena. During
jumping routines, her littlest would bounce
in her seat after horse and rider cleared the
hurdle. "Wow!" she would exclaim as she
gleefully clapped her tiny hands.

At one particular show Alice would always
remember, a young woman sat with remarkable poise and stunning elegance upon a
breath-taking black stallion. Alice couldn't
help but notice how her teenaged daughter
instinctively pulled her shoulders back
and sat up taller in her seat as horse and
rider passed.

Later Alice remarked, "I'm glad we were
able to give our kids a chance to see people
and animals at their best. It's a way, I hope,
of inspiring them to be, and do, their best
wherever life takes them."

Show Quality

What inspires you? If an awesome sunset takes your breath away, you will step outside in the late afternoon and scan the western sky. If classical music stirs your heart and soul, you will listen to it often and perhaps build a collection. You do this because these things lift your spirit and renew your love of life. They're what make you feel good about yourself and the world around you.

We move toward what inspires us. That's why it's good to evaluate those things we look toward for inspiration. It's good to ask ourselves if these things are leading us in the direction we want to go…if they encourage positive thinking and a healthy perspective on life…if they lead to God-pleasing goals and ideals.

The sights, sounds, books, movies, people, and places that inspire you become a part of your thoughts, hopes, and aspirations. They mold and shape you. That's why what inspires you is important to you… and to your God.

Place my heart and mind, dear God, on things of true beauty, goodness, and worthiness. Amen

It seems to me we can never give up
longing and wishing while we are
thoroughly alive. There are certain
things we feel to be beautiful
and good, and we must hunger
after them.
George Eliot

A grain thrown into good ground
brings forth fruit; a principle thrown
into a good mind brings forth fruit.
Everything is created and conducted
by the same Master—
the root, the branch, the fruits—
the principles, the consequences.
Blaise Pascal

Set your affection on things above,
not on things on the earth.
Colossians 3:2

Whatsoever things are true,
whatsoever things are honest,
whatsoever things are just,
whatsoever things are pure,
whatsoever things are lovely,
whatsoever things are of good report;
if there be any virtue, and if there be
any praise, think on these things.
Philippians 4:8

The pure, the beautiful, the bright,
  That stirred our hearts in youth,
The impulse to a wordless prayer,
  The dreams of love and truth,
The longings after something lost,
  The spirit's yearning cry,
The strivings after better hopes—
  These things can never die.

Sarah Doudney

Gentle, specially trained horses have given
countless children the experience of sitting
high in the saddle and feeling the strength
of well-honed muscles carrying them far
beyond where they could go themselves.
Many special needs kids have felt, for the
first time, the brush of wind against their
face. Others have gained a new sense of
control by learning how a slight pull of the
reins or gentle nudge of the foot can man-
age a creature so large and strong. They
discover fields and streams as their horse
carries them along, and traipse through
woodlands with a horse's powerful legs
beneath them.

When they grow up, they stand taller
and feel more confident than those who
have never known the freedom of galloping across field and meadow. The picture
of their favorite horse will never fail to
bring back memories of learning about the
world, themselves, and life.

True Freedom

If we know ourselves, we know our weaknesses. Not one of us has perfect knowledge and strength, and all of us at one time or another have made mistakes, lacked the skills we needed, and stumbled along the way.

Our God knows our weaknesses, yet no weakness of ours keeps Him from loving us. He not only feels compassion for us in our weaknesses, but He does something about them. He strengthens our faith, fortifies our hope, and gives us the ability to live according to His purpose. No longer weighed down by guilt or regret, we're free to live joyfully and productively.

The freedom God gives you opens a whole new world to you. In Him, you are not weak, but made strong in spirit...not bound by difficulties, but given wings of hope and trust...not incapable, but provided with everything you need to know and do His will. This is His freedom for you to savor, thrive in, and enjoy every day.

Free me, dear God, for everything that would hinder me from knowing You. Amen

Now the Lord is that Spirit:
and where the Spirit of the Lord is,
there is liberty.
2 Corinthians 3:17

Let me not be tied down to property
or praise and I shall be free.
Free from the nagging ache of envy.
Free from the hurts of resentment.
Free to love all and forgive all.
Free to do and say what is right,
regardless of the unpopularity.
Free to wander everywhere
as inspiration guides me.
Francis of Assisi

When you go to bed at night, have
for your pillow three things—love,
hope and forgiveness. And you will
awaken in the morning with
a song in your heart.
Victor Hugo

Stand fast therefore in the liberty
wherewith Christ hath made us free,
and be not entangled again with the
yoke of bondage.
Galatians 5:1

Resolve to be thyself;
and know that he who finds himself,
loses his misery.
Matthew Arnold

Only he who does nothing
makes no mistakes.
French proverb

Life appears to me too short
to be spent in nursing animosity or
registering wrong.
Charlotte Brontë

The troubles of my heart have
multiplied; free me from my anguish.
Psalm 25:17 NIV

Resentments are burdens
we don't need to carry.
Author unknown

Horses lend us the wings we lack.
Author unknown

The charm and quiet of the rural village
captivated the traveler. Carol spent the
afternoon exploring its narrow pathways
and taking pictures of quaint stone houses,
flower-pot lined balconies, and small,
carefully tended gardens. She stopped for
tea at a tiny outdoor café, where the pro-
prietor suggested she climb to the top of
the town's church tower. "You won't regret
it," the woman said. So Carol finished her
tea, went to the church, and found a door
opening to the winding stone stairway.

Once at the top, Carol gasped in awe.
There, just outside of town, stretched
fields where horses were grazing contentedly, some of the mares with their foals
standing close by them. The late afternoon shadows cast a poetic light on the
scene, and Carol lifted her camera.

Once home, Carol framed the picture.
She titled it "Serenity."

A Peaceful Place

Though we long for peace, the peace we seek can be elusive. We often attempt to find it by denying our problems, immersing ourselves in work, or escaping into addiction. Whatever peace these things may provide, however, is temporary, and brings additional difficulties.

True peace is God's peace. When you look to Him in prayer, you're in the presence of your heavenly Father who longs to embrace you in His love, compassion, and forgiveness. By meditating on His unfailing promise to be there for you at all times, to protect you, and to see you through every trouble, your anxieties slowly melt away. God's peace stills your spirit and fills your heart.

Peace is a blessing God longs to shower on you. It's a peace no one can take away. It is serenity designed to last a lifetime—and beyond.

Send Your Spirit into my life, dear God, and grant me the peace that brings true serenity of heart and soul. Amen

If you are inwardly free from
fighting, no one will be able
to start a fight with you.
Author unknown

Peace I leave with you, my peace I
give unto you: not as the world giveth,
give I unto you. Let not your heart be
troubled, neither let it be afraid.
John 14:27

Never be in a hurry; do everything
quietly and in a calm spirit. Do not
lose your inward peace for anything
whatsoever, even if your whole
world seems upset.
Francis de Sales

Cheerfulness keeps up a kind of
daylight in the mind, and fills it with a
steady and perpetual serenity.
Joseph Addison

To win true peace, a man needs to
feel directed, pardoned,
and sustained by a supreme power.
Henri F. Amiel

The peace of God, which passeth all understanding, shall keep your hearts and minds through Christ Jesus.
Philippians 4:7

People look in vain places for peace. They seek it in the world outside, in places, people, ways, activities.... They are looking in the wrong direction, and the longer they look the less they find what they are looking for.
Meister Eckhart

He maketh me to lie down in green pastures: he leadeth me beside the still waters.
Psalm 23:2

Where there is peace and meditation, then there is neither anxiety nor doubt.
Francis of Assisi

Within you there is a stillness and a sanctuary to which you can retreat at any time and be yourself.
Hermann Hesse

*The splendor of horses goes far beyond
their energy and appearance, their
strength and size. That's what their caring
human owners and companions learn as
they get to know a special animal over the
course of time. They discover, beneath the
whinnies and neighs, an individual person-
ality. They find their horse has an aptitude
for prancing or jumping or running, and
they guide the animal in doing what he
does best.*

*Communicating with a horse takes time
and patience, and good caretakers know
this. Letting the horse get to know his
humans is as important as it is for his
humans to get to know the horse.
A horse's well-being depends on it,
as well as the safety of everyone around
him. The reward comes when the bond
between owner and horse is so close that
one seems to know, at a mere glance,
the other's thoughts and feelings.*

Bond of Understanding

When there's a problem in a relationship, we usually can trace it back to miscommunication. Perhaps someone hasn't been listening, or has picked up the wrong message. Maybe one person won't take the time to understand another, or is incapable of doing so. Any one of these things can leave us frustrated and angry!

Good communication takes patience—patience with ourselves as we recognize and admit our mistakes. Our patience prompts us to listen more deeply, more carefully; and to have patience with others when they have not listened deeply or carefully to us.

Good communication with God takes patience, too. Though He knows everything about you, you do not know everything about Him. It takes patience on your part as He reveals Himself to you in His own time and in His own way. The longer you express your thoughts to Him and allow Him to touch your life and heart, the deeper and stronger your communication grows.

Dear God, enable me to better understand Your will as I walk closer to You each day. Amen

The first proof of a well-ordered
mind is to be able to pause
and linger with itself.
Seneca

The philosophy of waiting is sustained
by all the oracles of the universe.
Ralph Waldo Emerson

Hear the other side.
Augustine

Wait on the LORD: be of good
courage, and he shall strengthen
thine heart: wait, I say,
on the LORD.
Psalm 27:14

A handful of patience is worth more
than a bushel of brains.
Dutch proverb

The more elaborate our means
of communication,
the less we communicate.
Joseph Priestly

For now we see through a glass,
darkly; but then face to face:
now I know in part; but then shall
I know even as also I am known.
1 Corinthians 13:12

First learn the meaning of what you say,
and then speak.
Epictetus

To listen well is as powerful
a means of communication and
influence as to talk well.
John Marshall

He who does not understand
your silence will probably not
understand your words.
Elbert Hubbard

Electric communication will never be
a substitute for the face of someone
who with their soul encourages
another person to be brave and true.
Charles Dickens

Whenever their schedules permitted, Rose
and David would ride their horses together,
first in one direction from the stable, then
in another direction, until they had explored
all the trails except one. The untried trail
wound up a rocky slope and ended at a
lookout on top of the hill.

The day they decided to tackle it started
out warm and sunny, but once they arrived
at the lookout, a storm started rolling in.
They didn't have time to make it back down
before rain started, so they looked for
cover. There it was—a shallow shelter dug
into the side of the hill, large enough to
accommodate them and their animals.

"Even the horses know it's safe in here,"
remarked Rose. "Look how calm they are!"

After the storm passed, Rose and David
began their ride downhill as the welcome
sight of a rainbow spread across the sky.

Shelter

Life's storms can come suddenly and unexpectedly. Financial difficulties crush our plans…a medical diagnosis shifts our priorities…a family tragedy shatters our expectations.

Though God does not always choose to take us out of the storm, we can depend on Him to provide shelter during the storm. He offers assurance of His presence as we face the situation, and He provides the strength we need to bear up under the burden of hardship and pain. Each day we confront the danger around us, God is there with His compassion, His wisdom, and His peace. In the shelter of His love, we stand safe.

When the storm has passed and the skies are blue once again, we discover that we have changed. We're stronger, more confident, and closer to God than ever before. The skies look clearer and the sun feels brighter because we know we can handle the clouds. And that's a promise!

Dear God, be with me in my struggles and take me into the shelter of Your compassion and peace. Amen

You cannot create experience.
You must undergo it.
Albert Camus

If the sky falls, hold up your hands.
Spanish proverb

God is our refuge and strength,
a very present help in trouble.
Therefore will not we fear, though
the earth be removed, and though
the mountains be carried into the
midst of the sea.
Psalm 46:1-2

Life is my college. May I graduate
well, and earn some honors!
Louisa May Alcott

Affliction comes to us all,
not to make us sad, but sober,
not to make us sorry, but wise,
not to make us despondent,
but by the darkness to refresh us.
Henry Ward Beecher

Have mercy on me, my God,
have mercy on me, for in you I
take refuge. I will take refuge in the
shadow of your wings until
the disaster has passed.
Psalm 57:1 NIV

The habits of a vigorous mind are
formed in contending with difficulties.
Abigail Adams

And the Lord shall deliver me from
every evil work, and will preserve me
unto his heavenly kingdom.
2 Timothy 4:18

Misfortune is never mournful to the soul
that accepts it; for such do always see
that in every cloud is an angel's face.
Jerome

I have had more than half a century
of such happiness. A great deal of
worry and sorrow, too, but never a
worry or a sorrow that was not offset
by a purple iris, a lark, a bluebird, or
a dewy morning glory.
Mary McLeod Bethune

*The will of God will not
take you where the grace
of God cannot keep you.*
Saying

**Adversity has ever been considered
the state in which a man most easily
becomes acquainted with himself.**
Samuel Johnson

*Take unto you the whole armor
of God, that ye may be able to
withstand in the evil day, and having
done all, to stand.*
Ephesians 6:13

**If I had a formula for bypassing
trouble, I would not pass it round.
Trouble creates a capacity to handle it.
I don't embrace trouble; that's as bad
as treating it as an enemy. But I do say
meet it as a friend, for you'll see a lot
of it and had better be on speaking
terms with it.**
Oliver Wendell Holmes

*God gives us always strength
enough, and sense enough, for
everything He wants us to do.*
John Ruskin

I know God will not give me anything
I can't handle. I just wish that He
didn't trust me so much.
Mother Teresa

He shall give his angels charge over
thee, to keep thee in all thy ways.
They shall bear thee up in their hands,
lest thou dash thy foot against a stone.
Psalm 91:11-12

Smooth seas do not
make skillful sailors.
African proverb

If we had no winter, the spring would
not be so pleasant; if we did not
sometimes taste of adversity, prosperity
would not be so welcome.
Anne Bradstreet

There is in every true woman's heart
a spark of heavenly fire, which lies
dormant in the broad daylight of
prosperity; but which kindles up,
and beams and blazes in the dark
hour of adversity.
Washington Irving

"Look ahead!" her dad would call back to
her as he rode his horse, Ranger. Amy,
following on her pony, Tinkerbell, would
spot the low-hanging branch and duck,
just as her dad was doing ahead of her.
"Never gallop when you can't see what's
in front of you," he repeatedly warned
his daughter.

One day, Amy was particularly eager to
visit her friend on a neighboring farm, and
she saddled Tinkerbell. "Be careful," her
dad called out. "It stormed last night!"

"Right!" said Amy. As she entered the
woods, she took a deep breath of the
fresh, clean air. Exhilarated, she nudged
Tinkerbell into a gallop. She never saw
the branch that nearly knocked her out
of the saddle. The goose egg on her head
was clear evidence of what had happened,
and she was forced to say the words
parents love to hear: "You were right."

Whoa!

For all of us, there have been times we haven't taken good advice...when we've hurried on, heedless of warnings...when we've run into trouble because we didn't look ahead. Caution is a lesson most of us learn from sad experience, and as we mature, we're generally more likely to think before we act.

In the Bible, our all-knowing God offers us His counsel and His cautions. For our spiritual growth and maturity, He provides the experience of both those who have listened to His words and those who have ignored it. He warns us not to take paths that would lead us away from Him, and He teaches us to look out for temptations that can easily fell us if we do not pay attention.

The more you stop to hear God speak to you in the words of Scripture, the more you're able to look ahead—and go ahead—with joy and confidence.

Teach me, dear God, to stop and listen to You, and to obey Your wise counsel in everything I do. Amen

Advice is like snow; the softer it falls
the longer it dwells upon, and the
deeper it sinks into the mind.
Samuel Coleridge

When a man has been guilty of any
vice or folly, the best atonement he
can make for it is to warn others not to
fall into the like.
Joseph Addison

Hear instruction, and be wise,
and refuse it not.
Proverbs 8:33

To accept good advice is but to
increase one's own ability.
Johann Wolfgang von Goethe

No man is so foolish but he may
sometimes give another good coun-
sel, and no man so wise that he may
not easily err if he takes no other
counsel than his own.
Ben Jonson

I will praise the LORD,
who counsels me; even at night my
heart instructs me.
Psalm 16:7 NIV

**He that gives good advice, builds with
one hand; he that gives good counsel
and example, builds with both.**
Francis Bacon

Therefore whosoever heareth these
sayings of mine, and doeth them,
I will liken him unto a wise man,
which built his house upon a rock:
And the rain descended, and the floods
came, and the winds blew,
and beat upon that house; and it fell not:
for it was founded upon a rock.
Matthew 7:24-25

**We are apt to be very pert
at censuring others, where we will not
endure advice ourselves.**
William Penn

Miniature horses might measure no larger than a German shepherd. Like German shepherds, they can be trained as Guide Horses for visually impaired people. Well-mannered miniature horses are also fine companion animals and ideal pets for households with a lot of room and a lot of love to give.

Like all horses, miniatures relish having a place outdoors where they can relax and play. When indoors, some miniatures follow their owners around the house. Others prefer to laze on the couch or snuggle in their favorite chair. Though not as needy of affection as dogs, miniature horses like to be groomed, scratched, and petted by their humans.

Though they're little, don't be fooled—a miniature horse has a stallion-sized heart full of love to share!

A Big Heart

A big heart delivers small kindnesses. You don't need to spearhead major projects, but only be there for those everyday "minor" acts of generosity, such as responding kindly to others' needs, both spoken and unspoken. Your money isn't required, only your time... time spent giving others your attention, consideration, and care.

The small kindnesses we receive from God each day so often go unnoticed, yet our big-hearted God continues to shower us with His blessings. His kindness is the source of our material blessings, like food and shelter, clothing and comfort; and spiritual blessings, like joy, peace, and love. Even more: He always has time for us when we call to Him in thought, speech, and prayer. The big-hearted generosity of our God has no limits!

Yes, huge life-changing miracles come from His hand, but so do all the daily blessings and small favors that warm and gladden your heart.

Thank You, dear God, for all the blessings You put into my every day. Amen

The eyes of all wait upon thee;
and thou givest them their meat
in due season. Thou openest thine
hand, and satisfies the desire of
every living thing.
Psalm 145:15-16

**Little things are indeed little, but to be
faithful in little things is a great thing.**
Augustine

Blessed be the God and Father
of our Lord Jesus Christ,
who hath blessed us with all
spiritual blessings in
heavenly places in Christ.
Ephesians 1:3

**We ourselves feel that what we are
doing is just a drop in the ocean. But if
that drop was not in the ocean, I think
the ocean would be less because of
that missing drop. I do not agree with
the big way of doing things.**
Mother Teresa

The spirit of delight
comes in small ways.
Robert Louis Stevenson

**That man is happiest who lives from
day to day and asks no more,
garnering the simple goodness of life.**
Euripides

What shall I render unto the LORD
for all his benefits toward me?
Psalm 116:12

**Life is made up not of great sacrifices
or duties, but of little things,
in which smiles, and kindnesses,
and small obligations,
given habitually are what win and
preserve the heart and secure comfort.**
Humphry Davy

*The summer before his third year in college,
Marvin stayed at his grandparents' house
and helped his grandfather on the farm.
It was there that he first spotted a pretty
blonde girl with a regal bearing riding a
dappled mare along the path between the
fields. "Ahh, what would she want with a
hay-seed like me?" he thought. Though he
saw her several times, he never dared to ask
who she was or introduce himself.*

*That fall, he returned to the apartment on
campus he shared with his roommate, Scott.
"Hey, Marv," Scott said the first day back.
"It's my kid sister's first year here. Want to
come along while I show her around?"*

*Marvin did, and he recognized her immedi-
ately as the girl on the dappled mare. She
had been staying with an aunt who lived
in town the summer he had seen her. On
their sixtieth wedding anniversary, Marvin
still chuckled to remember how he met his
beloved wife!*

God in Action

Just a coincidence, or God at work? How blessed are those who are able to recognize the hand of God in all creation and give Him thanks for all He does!

Think about the special people that have come into your life and the great opportunities that have come your way. Could you have planned these things? Could you have made them happen? Probably not! Rather, a chain of events far outside your influence and control resulted in a certain person crossing your path…
the chance of a lifetime being offered to you…
a single, unforeseen event turning your life in a new, exciting direction.

We like to go after what we want, and we pride ourselves on creating our own opportunities and taking advantage of whatever resources we possess. And God rewards our efforts. But when it comes to what He has in mind for us, nothing can stand in His way. That's God in action.

Dear God, thank You for all the things You have made happen in my life. Amen

*A door that seems to stand open
must be a man's size, or it is not the
door that Providence means for him.*
Henry Ward Beecher

**Destiny grants us our wishes,
but in its own way, in order to give us
something beyond our wishes.**
Johann Wolfgang von Goethe

*The mind controlled
by the Spirit is life and peace.*
Romans 8:6 NIV

**There's a divinity that shapes our
ends, rough-hew them how we will.**
William Shakespeare

Is any thing too hard for the LORD?
Genesis 18:14

All things are of God,
who hath reconciled us to himself
by Jesus Christ.
2 Corinthians 5:18

A person often meets his destiny on the road he took to avoid it.
Jean de La Fontaine

But now, O LORD,
thou art our father; we are the clay,
and thou our potter;
and we all are the work of thy hand.
Isaiah 64:8

Destiny itself is like a wonderful wide tapestry in which every thread is guided by an unspeakable tender hand, placed beside another thread and held and carried by a hundred others.
Rainer Maria Rilke

Clover came into Howard's life as a six-year-old. Howard's neighbors had bought him, but unfortunately, Clover didn't get along with the neighbor's other horses. Howard, a widower, noticed Clover and took a liking to him, so he suggested that Clover might prefer a stable and corral of his own. The men agreed on a price, and Clover came to live with Howard.

Howard soon realized that Clover did more than inhabit an empty stable at the back of his house. Each morning, Howard had a reason to get up…Clover needed feeding and grooming. Howard had a reason to get out of the house, because the stable needed cleaning and water needed freshening. For Clover's daily exercise, Howard rode him around the corral, across the meadow, and through the woods.

For the first in many years, Howard realized that, through Clover, he had found a quiet, agreeable happiness.

Happy Trails

Life's losses can make us feel like we'll never feel happy again. The pain is so deep and the anguish so intense that we can believe ourselves beyond the reach of cheerfulness.

While our losses lead us through darkness, God desires to draw us out again. The gift of time pulls us further and further from the hurt, and God's Spirit works in our heart to embrace us in faith and hope. He sends people and events into our lives to help us reach out, because God never takes away without giving back, according to His wisdom.

The definition of happiness changes many times throughout life. Sometimes it can be readily seen, and at other times we must look for it in its quieter, more subtle forms. Sometimes it's easily grasped, and other times we must wait for it with patience. Either way, happiness is ours through our faith, the source of all true joy.

Dear God, thank You for the happiness I have known. I look to You for my joy, now and forever. Amen

There is no duty we so much
underrate as the duty
of being happy.
Robert Louis Stevenson

A happy heart makes
the face cheerful.
Proverbs 15:13 NIV

True happiness is of a retired
nature, and an enemy to pomp and
noise; it arises, in the first place,
from the enjoyment of one's self,
and, in the next, from the
friendship and conversation
of a few select companions.
Joseph Addison

Happiness is not a horse—
you cannot harness it.
Asian proverb

Talk happiness. The world is sad
enough without your woe. No path
is wholly rough; look for the places
that are smooth and clear.
Ella Wheeler Wilcox

Be glad in the LORD, and rejoice.
Psalm 32:11

True happiness is to understand our duties toward God and man; to enjoy the present, without being anxious about the future; not to amuse ourselves with hopes and fears, but to rest satisfied with what we have.
Seneca

Happiness is a butterfly, which, when pursued, is always just beyond your grasp, but which, if you will sit down quietly, may alight upon you.
Nathaniel Hawthorne

The foolish seek happiness over the horizon; the wise find it under their feet.
Author unknown

Let us be glad and rejoice,
and give honour to him.
Revelation 19:7

Whoever possesses God is happy.
Augustine

Allan was a shy child, and by the time he entered middle school, he was lagging behind other students both academically and socially. He seemed uninterested in everything except horses, so Allan's parents took the advice of a school counselor and allowed him to take horseback riding lessons.

Over the course of the year, Allan showed remarkable progress. He had a natural affinity for the horses, and he quickly developed into a capable rider. His self-assurance swelled when he realized that other kids admired his skill, and his ability to master horsemanship gave him the confidence he needed to tackle subjects in school.

From that time on, Allan was never far from horses, whether as rider, groomer, trainer, or caretaker. He had found his talent and his pleasure, his satisfaction and his strength.

A Place of Bliss

While some of us have known exactly what we wanted to do in life from an early age, most of us find it by trial and error. By trying different subjects in school or various jobs in the workplace, we discover what we're good at and what we enjoy. It's there we find our niche in the world—where we discover our bliss.

God has blessed each of us with different strengths and talents, and He intends for us to use them. When we do, we find satisfaction with ourselves and with our life. We may not be in the same place or at the same level as someone else, and we might not get the acclaim that others do. But if we have found our bliss, we have found a God-given treasure.

Your pleasure of life begins with a realization that God has blessed you with unique talents, strengths, interests, gifts, and dreams. There is a place only you can fill.

Dear God, lead me to my bliss—the place of my satisfaction and delight. Amen

There are diversities of gifts,
but the same Spirit.
1 Corinthians 12:4

We know what we are,
but know not what we may be.
William Shakespeare

We only do well the
things we like doing.
Colette

Know that the greatest things which
are done on earth are done within,
in the hearts of faithful souls.
Louis de Montfort

There is just one life for each of us:
our own.
Euripides

You must be holy in the way God asks
you to be holy.
Vincent Pallotti

Do not wish to be
anything but what you are.
Francis de Sales

' Tis a gift to come round
to where we ought to be.
Appalachian folk song

Nature arms each man with some
faculty which enables him to do easily
some feat impossible to any other.
Ralph Waldo Emerson

Do not neglect your gift,
which was given you.
1 Timothy 4:14 NIV

The first duty of a human being is to
assume the right functional
relationship to society—more briefly,
to find your real job, and do it.
Charlotte Perkins Gilman

The chestnut mare thrived on racing. When her owner's van pulled up to take her to the track, she nickered and whinnied with excitement as she trotted smartly up the ramp of her trailer. During the trip, did she anticipate the noise of the crowds and the neighs of the other horses...the line-up at the gate and the sound of the starting bell? Once at the track, she was in her element.

Though she was a fit animal and an enthusiastic racer, the mare didn't always win. Sometimes she came in second or third; occasionally she lagged far behind the fastest horses. Yet each time, she ran with all her might, and her owner knew that. Whether she won or lost, he gave her a pat and a treat before their trip home. "Good girl," he'd say. "You gave 'em your best. Good girl!"

A Winning Effort

The successes of others often motivate us to try harder, to reach further, and to excel. Without the healthy competition others provide, many of us would fall far below our potential. Winning, however, is not our goal, and it's not what God asks of us. Rather, our goal, and God's will, is that we give what we do our best effort.

God's pleasure comes equally to all who faithfully run the race ahead of them, whether they "win" status and fame in the world or they remain unnoticed. He delights in those who walk close to Him without wavering, even if the path leads away from what the world values and rewards. God's approval rests with a heart willing to persevere in faith, hope, and love of life.

The Spirit of God at work in our heart is the source of lasting emotional strength and energy. It's always there for those who call on Him...it's available to all who faithfully run the race each day.

Enable me, dear God, to enter each day with excitement and gratitude. Amen

The LORD preserveth the faithful.
Psalm 31:23

A horse never runs so fast
as when he has other horses to catch
up and outpace.
Ovid

God doesn't require us to succeed,
he only requires that you try.
Mother Teresa

Enthusiasm is the greatest
asset in the world. It is nothing more
or less than faith in action.
Henry Chester

When a man's willing and eager,
God joins in.
Aeschylus

Knowing is not enough,
we must apply. Willing is not enough,
we must do.
Johann Wolfgang von Goethe

*And what doth the LORD require of
thee, but to do justly,
and to love mercy,
and to walk humbly with thy God?*
Micah 6:8

**It is only when I dally with what I am
about, look back and aside instead of
keeping my eyes straight forward, that
I feel these cold sinkings of the heart.**
Sir Walter Scott

Honor lies in the mane of a horse.
Herman Melville

**O Lord, thou givest us everything,
at the price of an effort.**
Leonardo da Vinci

*Jellybean bounded into the pasture.
She galloped several times around its
perimeter, and then stubbornly planted
herself at the far end. I had been warned
she was a willful horse, but just how
willful I learned when I tried to bring
her into the barn at the end of the day.*

*Clearly, Jellybean did not want to be
caught. Whenever I headed toward her,
she galloped as far away from me as possible. So I didn't insist she come to me or
into the barn. Instead, I walked around
the enclosure and let her get used to me.
Soon, she started moving closer to me...
checking me out, I guess. Still, I didn't
grab her. I waited.*

*After only a few weeks, she stood still
and let me stroke her. Not long after, she
accepted a halter and lead. Now Jellybean
was ready—and willing—to receive my
friendship and love.*

Love of a Lifetime

Where genuine love is present, there is no force or compulsion. Instead, genuine love desires only freely given love in return. Genuine love is willing to wait; genuine love draws love by being patient, kind, and attentive, because that's the way love is.

God's love for you is genuine, and that's why He never insists you turn to Him if you do not wish to do so. If you are afraid of faith's commitment, God allows you to exercise the faith you have as you ask questions and learn more. God will delight in hearing your voice, whether through a traditional prayer or in a few words spoken from your heart.

Yes, God desires your love because He loves you with deep, limitless love. His Son came into the world to show you the meaning of His love. Whenever you respond to His love, He will be there, for He's always ready to respond to you.

Help me, dear God, open my heart and mind to the great love You offer to me. Amen

For God so loved the world,
that he gave his only begotten Son,
that whosoever believeth in him
should not perish,
but have everlasting life.
John 3:16

**Love is our highest word
and the synonym for God.**
Ralph Waldo Emerson

I love, and the world is mine!
Florence Earle Coates

**'Tis sweet to know there is an eye
will mark our coming,
and look brighter when we come.**
Lord Byron

*You can give without loving, but you
can never love without giving.*
Robert Louis Stevenson

**Love is a fruit in season at all times,
and within the reach of every hand.**
Mother Teresa

God is love.
1 John 4:8

**To love anyone is nothing else than
to wish that person good.**
Thomas Aquinas

*Love withers under constraints;
its very essence is liberty;
it is compatible neither with
obedience, jealousy, nor fear.*
Percy Bysshe Shelley

Love is patient, love is kind.
1 Corinthians 13:4 NIV

*The supreme happiness of life is the
conviction that we are loved—
loved for ourselves, or rather,
loved in spite of ourselves.*
Victor Hugo

For inexperienced horse lovers, eagerness
to approach an animal and jump in the
saddle is usually mixed with some amount
of timidity. A horse is adept at detecting
fear, however, and will try to wrest control
from the human to himself. He'll exert
his authority by snorting and bucking and
making himself a challenge to mount and
unwieldy to ride. Trainers stress the impor-
tance of asserting authority over the animal
for a positive and productive relationship.

Though the horse's leader and manager,
the human also is responsible for the
animal's emotional and physical needs.
Fresh water and nutritional food, clean
shelter, proper grooming, and meaning-
ful companionship are a horse's minimum
daily requirements, and he depends on his
owner to provide them. While a "boss,"
a caring and compassionate owner acts
as a servant, too.

Reined In with Love

In the Bible, God reveals Himself as the originator of all things, and rightfully claims authority over creation. The inspired writers describe Him as a great, powerful, and all-holy king who insists on obedience to His commandments. If this is all we knew about God, we would have every reason to dread His presence!

When we read further, however, we discover more about who God is. We learn that He cares about the world and the people in it...that He responds to our prayers with forgiveness, gentleness, and understanding...that He desires to lead us into a loving, peaceful, and productive relationship with Him. God draws us to Himself as we put our faith in Him and rely on Him for all our daily needs.

God is king, but also a servant. He reigns far above us, but also within us. He is our all-powerful God who comes to us with kindness and love.

Help me, dear God, to understand more about Your splendor and power...Your gentleness and love. Amen

If I then, your Lord and Master,
have washed your feet;
ye also ought to wash one another's feet.
For I have given you an example, that ye
should do as I have done to you.
John 13:14-15

**The princes among us are those who
forget themselves and serve mankind.**
Woodrow Wilson

I am among you as he that serveth.
Luke 22:27

**There is nothing small
in the service of God.**
Francis de Sales

At the heart of silence is prayer.
At the heart of prayer is faith.
At the heart of faith is life.
At the heart of life is service.
Mother Teresa

No one is useless in this world who
lightens the burdens of another.
Charles Dickens

No one possesses spiritual maturity
until they have found it finer to serve
someone else than to serve themselves.
Author unknown

By love serve one another.
Galatians 5:13

Those who do not know how to serve
cannot know how to command.
English proverb

Doing nothing for others
is the undoing of ourselves.
Horace Mann

*I've heard some say how hard it is to meet
people, but it happens naturally when you
have a horse. See another owner at the
stable, and you have an instant topic of
conversation: horses! At shows, you can
talk to anyone because you know they're a
horse lover, just like you.*

*When I'm riding the trails and cross paths
with another rider, we smile and nod, and
often stop to talk about our animals. Then
we start chatting about the weather...the
scenery...our favorite food...and before
we know it, I'm sitting down to have dinner with them at a great new restaurant.*

*With a horse, it's never hard to meet
people...and not just people, but the
most fun, interesting, and caring people
in the world!*

Beneath the Surface

It's exciting to meet another person who shares our interests and passions. Immediately, we have something to talk about as we get to know each other, and so often we find many other shared points of agreement, conviction, and attitude. Mutual understanding, trust, and friendship develop. It's then we begin to share with each other deeper things, like our worries... our troubles...our sorrows.

So often, we're astonished to find that the smart, competent woman we admire suffers from nagging doubt and fear. We never would have guessed that the jovial, easy-going man we enjoy talking to is still mourning the passing of his beloved wife. Under the exterior— the face we see—we discover a burdened heart, just like ours.

Beneath surface appearances, we share hurts and regrets, troubles and hardships. They are ties we share in common. That's why compassion, kindness, and love never fail to bring us closer together.

Dear God, help me understand the needs of others and respond with true compassion and understanding. Amen

It is the province of knowledge to
speak and it is the privilege
of wisdom to listen.
Oliver Wendell Holmes

Rejoice with them that do rejoice,
and weep with them that weep.
Romans 12:15

Could a greater miracle take place
than for us to look through each
other's eye for an instant?
Henry David Thoreau

True kindness presupposes
the faculty of imagining as one's own
the suffering and joys of others.
André Gide

Bear ye one another's burdens,
and so fulfil the law of Christ.
Galatians 6:2

*Show mercy and compassion
to one another.*
Zechariah 7:9 NIV

**Taught by time,
my heart has learned to glow for
other's good, and melt at other's woe.**
Homer

*Kindness is a golden chain by which
society is bound together.*
Johann Wolfgang von Goethe

**Let the peace of Christ rule in your
hearts, since as members of one body
you were called to peace.**
Colossians 3:15 NIV

The Browns describe themselves as a horsey family. When great-grandfather Brown and his wife settled in the Midwest, they brought with them two horses, both pulling the wagon that held all their earthly possessions. Mr. Brown built a house and a stable on his land and acquired more horses, which he used for plowing and for taking his produce to market.

He had a knack for maintaining his herd's health, and soon neighbors sought him out for help with sick and injured animals. Brown's son became a large animal veterinarian, and his sons and daughters grew up riding and caring for horses. On their family tree are veterinarians and rodeo riders, trainers and groomers. Ribbons won by many of their beloved animals cover the wall of their den.

For each member of the family today, horses are a part of their lives... and their history.

A Godly Family

Many of us have had the privilege of growing up surrounded by aunts and uncles, grandparents and cousins. Others of us grew up in cities and towns far from our relatives, and distance prevented us from getting to know them well. But no matter which group we fall into, there's one family we're part of—the family of God.

The story of God's family goes back to ancient times and is still being told today as we remember all the things He has done for people in the past. We recall His movements throughout history, and we share with all believers the blessing of knowing we belong to Him. And because we belong to Him, we also belong to one another. Truly, we are brothers and sisters, mothers and fathers to each other because of God, our heavenly Father.

Dear God, thank You for being my Father in heaven. Thank you for all my brothers and sisters who share the bond of faith. Amen

And he stretched forth his hand
toward his disciples, and said,
Behold my mother and my brethren!
For whosoever shall do the will of my
Father which is in heaven, the same is
my brother, and sister, and mother.
Matthew 12:49-50

**What greater thing is there for human
souls than to feel that they are joined
for life...to be one with each other in
silent unspeakable memories.**
George Eliot

It is not flesh and blood
but the heart which makes us
fathers and sons.
Johann Schiller

**My sheep hear my voice,
and I know them, and they follow me.**
John 10:27

History is a cyclic poem written by
time upon the memories of man.
Percy Bysshe Shelley

My story would not be complete
without mentioning the people who
have meant the most to me,
the things I have cherished, and the
beloved horses that have been a
sweet, sustaining presence in my life.
T. J. Highland

God is faithful,
by whom ye were called
unto the fellowship of his Son
Jesus Christ our Lord.
1 Corinthians 1:9

How could we be strangers if we're
both following the Lord?
Saying

We will not hide them from their
children, shewing to the generation to
come the praises of the LORD,
and his strength, and his wonderful
works that he hath done.
Psalm 78:4

A fabric wall hanging occupies one wall of Linda's sewing room. It depicts three mares galloping gracefully across a gently sloping meadow. The horses—a golden bay with ebony mane and tail…a creamy Arabian…a spotted paint—are creatively and skillfully crafted with hand-dyed fabrics and embroidered with rich silk threads. Graduated greens in the fore-ground and a subtle rosy glow in the horizon embrace the bucolic scene.

"I feel the horses' vibrant energy whenever I look at this wall hanging," Linda says. "In my mind's eye, I can see them running, free and beautiful. I think of all the gorgeous horses I have known and the ones in my life right now. They never cease to lift my heart. They inspire me to let my creativity flow freely and flower into something beautiful."

Blessing of Life

Imagine fine horses grazing in the distance under a clear, cloudless sky. Put yourself standing next to a rough-hewn log fence and taking in the scene...feeling the warmth of buttery sunshine...breathing in spring-scented grasses and wildflowers...hearing the rustle of a gentle wind through the branches of a nearby oak. For many of us, just thinking of such a peaceful and picturesque scene makes us feel good about life and about ourselves!

God spreads His creation before us for us to admire and enjoy, and He has designed it to inspire us, to lift us up, and to surround us with beauty. In every sunrise, there's a whole new day of discovery...in every ancient tree, a reminder of God's shelter and preservation...in every new blossom, the hope that new life brings into the world.

There is splendor all around you, and God is the artist. He has blessed you with the gift of life and abundant promise it holds every single day.

Thank You, dear God, for the beauty of Your creation and for the gift of life. Amen

Nature is painting for us,
day after day, pictures of infinite
beauty if only we have the eyes
to see them.
John Ruskin

Since the creation of the world God's
invisible qualities—his eternal power
and divine nature—have been clearly
seen, being understood from
what has been made, so that people
are without excuse.
Romans 1:20 NIV

A horse is poetry in motion.
Author unknown

Never lose an opportunity of seeing
anything that is beautiful; for beauty
is God's handwriting—a wayside
sacrament. Welcome it in every fair
face, in every fair sky, in every fair
flower, and thank God for it as a
cup of blessing.
Ralph Waldo Emerson

To sit in the shade on a fine day
and look upon verdure
is the most perfect refreshment.
Jane Austen

*God writes the gospel not in the
Bible alone, but on trees and
flowers and clouds and stars.*
Martin Luther

**In all ranks of life the human heart
yearns for the beautiful;
and the beautiful things that God
makes are his gift to all alike.**
Harriet Beecher Stowe

*The heavens declare
the glory of God; the firmament
sheweth his handywork.*
Psalm 19:1

A thing of beauty is a joy forever.
John Keats

*If I were to name the three most
precious resources of life,
I would say books, friends and
nature; and the greatest of these,
at least the most constant and
always at hand, is nature.*
John Burroughs

*If you wish to advance
into the infinite,
explore the finite
in all directions.*
Johann Wolfgang von Goethe